SMALL GROUP SERIES

Transformation

LETTING GOD CHANGE YOU FROM THE INSIDE OUT

Interactions Small Group Series:

Authenticity: Being Honest with God and Others
Character: Reclaiming Six Endangered Qualities
Commitment: Developing Deeper Devotion to Christ
Community: Building Relationships Within God's Family
Evangelism: Becoming Stronger Salt and Brighter Light
Freedom: Breaking the Chains that Bind You
Fruit of the Spirit: Living the Supernatural Life
Jesus: Seeing Him More Clearly
Lessons on Love: Following Christ's Example
Marriage: Building Real Intimacy
Parenthood: Rising to the Challenge of a Lifetime
Prayer: Opening Your Heart to God
Psalms: Deepening Your Relationship with God
The Real You: Discovering Your Identity in Christ
Transformation: Letting God Change You from the Inside Out
Transparency: Discovering the Rewards of Truth-Telling

INTERActions

SMALL GROUP SERIES

Transformation

LETTING GOD CHANGE YOU FROM THE INSIDE OUT

BILL HYBELS

WITH KEVIN & SHERRY HARNEY

WILLOW CREEK

RESOURCES

ZONDERVAN

GRAND RAPIDS, MICHIGAN 49530

ZONDERVAN

Transformation
Copyright © 1997 by the Willow Creek Association

Requests for information should be addressed to:

Zondervan, *Grand Rapids, Michigan 49530*

ISBN: 0-310-21317-7

All Scripture quotations, unless otherwise indicated, are taken from the *Holy Bible: New International Version*®. NIV®. Copyright © 1973, 1978, 1984 by International Bible Society. Used by permission of Zondervan Publishing House. All rights reserved.

Interior design by Rick Devon

Printed in the United States of America

02 03 04 05 06 /❖ CH/ 15 14 13 12

CONTENTS

INTERACTIONS

In 1992, Willow Creek Community Church, in partnership with Zondervan Publishing House and the Willow Creek Association, released a curriculum for small groups entitled the *Walking with God* series. In just three years, almost a half million copies of these small group study guides were being used in churches around the world. The phenomenal response to this curriculum affirmed the need for relevant and biblical small group materials.

At the writing of this curriculum, there are over 1,500 small groups meeting regularly within the structure of Willow Creek Community Church. We believe this number will increase as we continue to place a central value on small groups. Many other churches throughout the world are growing in their commitment to small group ministries as well, so the need for resources is increasing.

In response to this great need, the *Interactions* small group series has been developed. Willow Creek Association and Zondervan Publishing House have joined together to create a whole new approach to small group materials. These discussion guides are meant to challenge group members to a deeper level of sharing, to create lines of accountability, to move followers of Christ into action, and to help group members become fully devoted followers of Christ.

SUGGESTIONS FOR INDIVIDUAL STUDY

1. Begin each session with prayer. Ask God to help you understand the passage and to apply it to your life.
2. A good modern translation, such as the New International Version, the New American Standard Bible, or the New Revised Standard Version, will give you the most help. Questions in this guide are based on the New International Version.
3. Read and reread the passage(s). You must know what the passage says before you can understand what it means and how it applies to you.
4. Write your answers in the spaces provided in the study guide. This will help you to express clearly your understanding of the passage.
5. Keep a Bible dictionary handy. Use it to look up unfamiliar words, names, or places.

SUGGESTIONS FOR GROUP STUDY

1. Come to the session prepared. Careful preparation will greatly enrich your time in group discussion.

2. Be willing to join in the discussion. The leader of the group will not be lecturing, but will encourage people to discuss what they have learned in the passage. Plan to share what God has taught you in your individual study.

3. Stick to the passage being studied. Base your answers on the verses being discussed rather than on outside authorities such as commentaries or your favorite author or speaker.

4. Try to be sensitive to the other members of the group. Listen attentively when they speak, and be affirming whenever you can. This will encourage more hesitant members of the group to participate.

5. Be careful not to dominate the discussion. By all means participate! But allow others to have equal time.

6. If you are the discussion leader, you will find additional suggestions and helpful ideas in the Leader's Notes.

ADDITIONAL RESOURCES AND TEACHING MATERIALS

At the end of this study guide you will find a collection of resources and teaching materials to help you in your growth as a follower of Christ. You will also find resources that will help your church develop and build fully devoted followers of Christ.

Letting God Change You from the Inside Out

In search of youth, beauty, and self-esteem, people are submitting in droves to the surgeon's scalpel for a new face or reshaped body. Never before have surgeons been able to do so much to change a person's appearance. They can correct sagging chins, crooked noses, floppy ears, and bags under eyes. They can make breasts larger or smaller, or put hair on a bald man's head. They can flatten abdomens or shrink thighs and buttocks. In the process, cosmetic surgery has become big business. Millions of people spend billions of dollars each year trying to make themselves more beautiful.

And the preoccupation with looking good does not stop there. Every year, Americans, most of them women, spend over ten billion dollars on cosmetics. Skin care products are more than a billion-dollar business as well. Every day people buy creams, lotions, and oils that promise the mythological rejuvenation that would come from a long soak in the fountain of youth.

Americans also spend millions on health foods, vitamins, diet and exercise books, diet drinks, barbells, aerobic and dance classes, and anything else that might give them an edge on looking their best. There are even super spas where you can go and spend two to three thousand dollars a week to have your body rejuvenated with massages, Roman baths, and two-hour facials.

The sad reality is that people will go to unbelievable lengths and pay incredible sums of money in order to become more physically desirable in the eyes of others. I believe that people are hoping that looking better will make them feel better about themselves. Maybe if the outside package looks better, then they won't hurt so much on the inside. Maybe then they can see themselves as worthwhile.

Amid all the clamor of pumping iron, dieting, jogging, exercising, being toned, tucked, tanned, and siliconed, the words of God's clear voice can barely be heard. But if you listen closely, you can hear Him say through the prophet in the Old Testament, "The LORD does not look at the things man looks at. Man looks at the outward appearance, but the LORD looks at the heart" (1 Sam. 16:7).

This does not mean that caring for our bodies is unimportant. Our bodies are temples of the Holy Spirit, and they need to be honored as the gifts of God they are. But we must be reminded that our bodies are not of ultimate importance. They are certainly not as important as matters of the heart. While most of us will go to incredible lengths to alter our exteriors in order to gain the approval of others, to what lengths will we go to alter our interiors in order to gain the approval of God?

It is God's nature to be concerned with the interior—with matters of the heart. The concept of the heart is used hundreds of times in the Bible. Most of the time, these references are not dealing with the organ that pumps blood through our veins and arteries, but to our nonphysical self—our mind, will, emotions, spirit, and personality. The heart is simply the core of our being. God is concerned with transforming us from the inside out!

> Therefore, if anyone is in Christ, he is a new creation; the old has gone, the new has come!
>
> *2 Corinthians 5:17*

> *Bill Hybels*

A New Heart

There is a very serious heart disease we should all know about. I call it "the disease of hard-heartedness." There is also a very painful but effective cure for this disease.

Many times in the Old Testament we read that God accused the people of Israel of being hard-hearted. In the New Testament, Jesus would sometimes tell the religious leaders, and even His own followers, "Your hearts are so hard!" In the Bible "hard-hearted" refers to the unresponsive, stiff, angry, insensitive, rebellious, and independent attitude ruling our hearts. This attitude is first directed toward God, but also toward other people.

Jesus told a parable of a farmer who went out and sowed seeds. You don't have to have a green thumb to know that the object of sowing seed is to get it into fertile soil so it can take root and produce fruit. Jesus pointed out that often when a farmer would throw seed, some would land on hard-packed soil. That seed was wasted; it would never grow. Jesus went on to explain what He meant by this agricultural story. Some people's hearts are impenetrable, hardened, unresponsive, and callous. The Word of God just bounces off. It doesn't even take root.

Soil = heart

Seed = word of God

If I were to nominate a biblical character for the "Iron Heart Award," I would submit the man who was crucified next to Jesus. When Jesus was nailed to the cross, there was a criminal being executed on His right and another on His left. One was a repentant thief. In the last moments of his life, he softened his heart and said, "Oh Lord, would You remember me?" Jesus said to him, "Today you'll be with Me in paradise." But the other thief, who was being crucified for a life of crime and violence, had a hard heart. He was minutes from death, inches from the Savior, but his heart was like stone. He was busy hurling abuse and insults at Jesus.

The repentant thief called over to the hard-hearted thief and said, "I can't believe it. You are minutes away from death and inches away from the Savior and you're still hard! Don't you fear God?" From all indications of Scripture, the "Iron Heart Award" would have been presented to that unrepentant thief on his arrival in hell. And that is what will happen ultimately to those people who spend their whole lives with an attitude of hard-heartedness.

A WIDE ANGLE VIEW

1 If you were a spiritual doctor doing a test for hard-heartedness, what are some of the symptoms you would look for in your examination?

A BIBLICAL PORTRAIT

Read Ezekiel 11:17–21; 36:24–28

2 According to Ezekiel, idolatry was a sign of hard-heartedness. What did idolatry look like in Ezekiel's day?

What does idolatry look like in our day?

unresponsive to God to His word
love of money   Romans 1:18
* self-sufficiency
de-sensitized to sin

3 In these passages, Ezekiel tells of some specific changes that are going to happen in the lives of God's people as their hearts are softened. What are some of these changes?

undivided heart
obedient " "
selflessness

value others opinions over God's
{ *desire for God* } *desire to be w/ other Christians*

In what ways are these same changes needed in our lives today if we are going to experience transformed hearts?

SHARPENING THE FOCUS

Read Snapshot "A Hard Heart"

A HARD HEART

Hearts get hard when we habitually say no to God. The very first time you say no to God a little layer forms around your heart. The second time another layer goes around your heart. The third time another layer forms, and on and on it goes. A person who ends up saying no to God for a lifetime ends up with a heart encased by steel.

As a person's heart grows hard, two things begin to happen. First, the hardness drives them farther away from God. There is no openness, no sensitivity to spiritual things, no desire to hear God speak. Hard hearts finally say, "I have no need for God or the things God has to offer." Second, when a heart grows hard, there is a lack of sensitivity toward others. Selfishness sets in and generosity is driven away. Other people become commodities, pawns in the game of life, a means to an end. True love in relationships and care for others is no longer a possibility for people with hearts lined with steel.

4

Describe a time in your life when you experienced hard-heartedness toward God. How did this impact your faith and relationship with Him?

5

During a time you were experiencing a hard heart toward God, what impact did this have on your relationships with *one* of the following people?

- A close friend
- A colleague at work
- Your spouse
- A family member

soft - heart
Go to God & ask what you can do - how can you make things better not look to other people.

Read Snapshot "A New Heart"

A New Heart

God says that if this disease is going to be dealt with, the first step is for the heart to be pierced . . . stabbed . . . pricked. In the book of Acts we read about the Day of Pentecost when Peter received the Holy Spirit and began to preach with great power (Acts 2:38). At the end of the message we read that all of the people who heard were "pierced in their hearts." They were stabbed with truth from the Word of God. Hebrews 4:12 says that the Bible is like a razor-sharp, double-edged sword . . . it cuts, stabs, pierces, and sometimes hurts. But it's the only hope for a hard heart.

The toughest truth for us to hear, the one that cuts the deepest, is the one we need to hear the most. The Bible tells us there is a root cause for hard-heartedness. The Bible calls it "sin." We're born in it. We're conceived in it. We have a sin nature, and we make sinful choices. We all have this heart disease. Romans 6:23 tells us that it is a terminal illness. All of us are infected with the disease of hard-heartedness toward God and others and we can't cure ourselves.

The good news is that God has a cure. The cure is miraculous. The cure is 100 percent effective. But, the cure is painful. No getting around it. The only way to get a new heart is to acknowledge your sin (that your heart is damaged beyond repair) and to let God forgive you and give you a new heart. There are no bypass surgeries, or simple solutions. It is going to take a heart transplant if we are going to experience change in our lives. It will be painful, but the new heart you receive will make all the difference in this life and for eternity!

6 If you have acknowledged your heart disease to God and received a new heart through Jesus Christ, how has this decision changed your life?

7 If you have not yet asked God for a new heart through Jesus, what is standing in the way of this decision?

What are some practical things we can do to help our heart stay sensitive to God.

1. Pray - ask

2. listen to His word *✱ Stay thankful*

3. commit God's word to our memory

Read Snapshot "A Soft Heart" *worship /sing*

A SOFT HEART

Part of having a new heart is having a soft heart toward others. In the New Testament days there was a man named Saul. Before he got his new heart, he used to intimidate followers of Christ, arrest them, beat them, and sometimes kill them. He thought he was doing the right thing, but his heart was hard as stone. But, hard-hearted Saul was pierced with the truth of Christ on the Damascus Road, and he received a heart transplant.

His responsiveness to God is legendary. His new heart became soft toward God and others. He soon referred to himself as a bond servant, a slave, and clay in God's hands. He became sensitive and soft toward other men and women. Old hard-hearted Saul became soft-hearted Paul. He ended up writing many of the books of the New Testament and his favorite term for other followers of Christ was, "Brothers and Sisters." He also called new Christians, "My dearly beloved little children." In Philippians 1:7 he simply says, "I have you in my heart." When we let God move in us, He will give us a soft heart toward others.

8 How have you seen God soften your heart toward others since you have become a follower of Christ?

9 Who is one person you need to soften your heart toward?

In what ways can your small group members pray for you and keep you accountable to honor Christ in this relationship?

PUTTING YOURSELF IN THE PICTURE

A SOFT AND RESPONSIVE HEART

When you have a new heart, you have a desire to be submissive to God. Every morning you need to say, "I give You my life today, Lord." You can start your day singing, "Have Your own way, Lord. Have Your own way. You are the potter, I am the clay." You begin to pray, "Mold me, make me, do whatever You want with my life, it's Yours." It's a submission issue, a flexibility issue, a surrender issue. Your life motto becomes: "Just say the word, Lord." Your soft heart says, "Whatever the Scriptures teach, that's what I want to do." A responsive heart is one that always says yes to the Holy Spirit.

Take time in prayer every morning for the coming week and offer your heart to God. Ask Him to soften your heart and make you responsive to His will and leading. Commit yourself to follow His will as He reveals it through Bible study, through experiences, and through the gentle promptings of His Holy Spirit.

PRAYING FOR OTHERS

Identify someone in your life who still has a hard heart toward God. Commit yourself to take at least five minutes every day for the next month to pray for this person's heart to soften toward God. Pray that they will recognize their own need for a spiritual "heart transplant" and pray for the Holy Spirit to begin doing surgery on them, even if it hurts.

Family

✳ Gods prompting me to......
3) spend more time w/ Him
3) build our relationship

A NEW MIND

REFLECTIONS FROM SESSION 1

1. If you have been taking time daily to pray for God to soften your heart, what changes have you been experiencing in your relationship with God and in your relationships with others?
2. If you have been consistently praying for a person in your life who is hard-hearted toward God, how has this impacted your relationship with that person? If you have seen the person's heart begin to change, describe what you are seeing.

THE BIG PICTURE

Some years ago I was invited to go flying with a professional pilot. It didn't take long to realize this was going to be an unusual flight. First, we went to the trunk of his car and he pulled out a parachute and strapped it on my back. And then, when we actually got into the plane, he used *six seat belts* to strap me into position behind him!

After we had gone up five thousand feet, the pilot asked me if I was ready for us to do a simple roll over the top. When he completed the roll, he turned back over his shoulder and said, "How was that? How are you feeling?"

"It was great," I replied. "I'm feeling fine." And then I said to myself, "Forgive me, Lord. It was just a small lie."

"So," the pilot then said, "are you ready for some other things?"

"Sure. I'm ready," I said. After all, what else are you going to say when you are strapped in the cockpit at five thousand feet?

We started doing a series of loops and other technical maneuvers. "This is going to be a hammerhead stall," he yelled. He pulled the plane straight up until it was ready to drop out of the air and then let it fall over to the side. We hurtled toward the ground. At that moment it felt like my eyeballs would go down into my stomach.

After every maneuver he would say, "How are you doing back there?" Each time I lied through my teeth and said, "I'm doing fine. Let's keep going."

As a grand finale, he turned the plane over and encouraged me to stay on the control stick while we flew upside down. There was a window over our heads, so we could see what was going on below us. This was a whole new sensation for me. He said, "If you stay with me on the stick you'll start to get the hang of it." Well, I stayed with him on the stick and I realized very quickly that all my prior years of flying and instruction were not of much value when flying upside down. I discovered that when a plane is flying upside down you do *everything in reverse*.

To bring this concept back to earth, imagine if someone altered the controls on your car so that left was right and right was left, or so that the gas pedal was the brake and the brake pedal the gas. What if forward was reverse and reverse forward? What would happen to your driving? It would take time for the old habits to change and for your mind to shift over to the new control patterns of your car. In the meantime, the roads would not be safe for anyone, including you!

A WIDE ANGLE VIEW

1   Take a moment and sign your name in the space below. Then print your name as clearly as you can below your signature:

Signature:

_____

Printed Name:

_____

Now, sign your name and print it with the other hand.
Try to do it as clearly as possible:

Signature:

_____

Printed Name:

_____

*How do you feel when you try to write with the hand you are
not used to using for writing?*

A BIBLICAL PORTRAIT

Read Romans 12:1–3

2 What are some of the "patterns of this world" that you
see people's minds conforming to?

3 In what ways do you see God's "good, pleasing and
perfect will" in conflict with the thinking of this world?

Read Snapshot "The Razor's Edge"

THE RAZOR'S EDGE

God wants all of us to live with mental tenacity as it pertains to our spiritual life. I remember these words from 1 Peter 1:13 when I was growing up: "Wherefore gird up the loins of your mind ..." (KJV). I used to think, *What in the world does that mean?* We don't talk about loins a whole lot these days, but back in the first century people knew what this term meant. Men wore long flowing robes and when there was a job to do or a foe to fight, they would take the bottom part of their robe and tuck it into their belt so they wouldn't trip on it. This was girding up the loins. In today's vernacular we might say, "Take off your coat and roll up your sleeves so you are ready for action."

"Gird up the loins of your minds" is another way of being told to prepare our minds for a fight. The Bible says we have to thoroughly retrain our minds if we are ever going to learn how to walk with Christ. As followers of Christ, we need to become critical thinkers. Even though we have had our minds renewed through salvation in Jesus Christ, we will spend the rest of our lives disciplining our minds, learning how they can become razor sharp. And when we think with the razor's edge, we begin to see things from God's perspective, not our own.

4

What are some of the things you have discovered that sharpen your thinking and help you see things from God's point of view?

5

What is one mental battle you are fighting now?

What are you doing to help you see things from God's vantage point and not as the world sees things?

Read Snapshot "The Ragged Edge"

THE RAGGED EDGE

Over time, many Christians' minds begin to focus on minor issues rather than on what is most important. New believers, after enjoying the initial thrill of becoming a Christ follower, can begin to settle into the routines of life. They no longer focus on the Great Problem-solver. Instead, their attention is diverted to the little problems of life.

A person who used to think often of heaven now thinks only of earth. While he used to marvel at the stockpile of blessings God has entrusted to His children, now he begins to look at what he *doesn't* have instead of what he does have. Over time, the vitality, joy, and excitement of his faith begins to fade. What has changed in this believer's life? Just one thing: He went from reasoning with a razor's edge to reasoning with a ragged edge.

---

6 Describe what your life was like during a time when you were thinking with the ragged edge instead of the razor's edge.

7 How have you seen the impact of ragged-edge thinking in *one* of these areas:

- Your view of yourself
- Your perspective on your marriage
- How you look at those who do not yet know the love of Jesus
- How you view your children
- How you use your free time

Read Snapshot "Sharpening the Edge"

SHARPENING THE EDGE

I want to give you three practical suggestions for how you can sharpen the ragged edge of thinking back to a razor's edge. First, saturate your mind with truth. Discover God's truth through personal Bible study, listening to biblical preaching, reading good Christian books, listening to tapes, and quality experiences and relationships. The key is to be sure to fill your mind with God's truth.

Second, submit yourself to the Holy Spirit. When you start moping around and crying over pocket change, the Spirit will remind you of your riches in Christ. He will whisper in your ear, "Don't think that way. Gird up the loins of your mind for battle. Fight against sloppy thinking. Think with a razor's edge." As you submit yourself to the Holy Spirit, you will make your mind available for the Spirit's warnings and promptings.

And third, build significant relationships with other followers of Christ. The Bible says that Christians need to sharpen one another. As you develop significant relationships with high-quality people who are committed to Christ, you will sharpen your thinking.

---

8 What are you doing on a daily or weekly basis to fill your mind with God's truth?

If you feel a need to deepen your commitment in this area of your spiritual life, how can your group members support you and keep you accountable?

9 Tell your group members about a person who is having a positive impact on your life by helping to sharpen you in your thinking.

What is it in that person's life and faith that inspires and challenges you?

PUTTING YOURSELF IN THE PICTURE

SHARPENING THE EDGE

Commit yourself to sharpen the edge of your thinking in one of the following ways:

- Spend at least fifteen minutes every day for one month reading the Bible. Have a group member pray for you, encourage you, and keep you accountable to follow through on this goal.
- Spend at least ten minutes each morning for two weeks listening quietly for the gentle leading of the Holy Spirit in your life. Ask God to give you His mind as you face the many decisions you will have to make in the day ahead.
- Identify one person who you respect as a committed follower of Christ. Contact that person and ask if you can spend time together in the coming month. Pray for God to use his or her life to sharpen yours.

NEW EARS

REFLECTIONS FROM SESSION 2

1. If you have been sharpening your thinking through regular study of the Bible, share what God has been teaching you.
2. If you have spent time with a follower of Christ who you respect, how has this helped to sharpen your faith?

THE BIG PICTURE

One day Jesus was by the seashore and some people began gathering to hear Him speak. Eventually there was such a crowd gathered that Jesus had to get into a boat and preach from just off the shoreline. After giving a very challenging and colorful moral message, Jesus said, "He who has ears, let him hear" (Matt. 13:9).

To our ears this may seem like a strange expression, but Jesus used it many times. "He who has ears to hear, let him hear." After a closer look at this expression, it becomes obvious what Jesus means. In fact, we all use similar expressions.

Imagine a mother yelling into the family room, "Jimmy, turn off the TV and get ready for bed." Jimmy says, "Okay," but it is clear that he has no intention of turning off the TV or going to bed. Instead, he stays right where he is . . . planted in front of the TV screen. Five minutes later she yells again, "Jimmy, did you hear me?" She knows he heard her because he had already responded by saying, "Okay!" What she's really asking when she says, "Did you hear me?" is whether Jimmy got the *point* of what she said. In this example, Jimmy apparently had heard his mother's voice, but not her point. You could almost hear her next words: "Hey, Jimmy! If those ears of yours are still working, turn that TV off and head upstairs!"

With crystal clarity Jesus was emphasizing that there is a lot more to hearing than simply receiving or intercepting a series of sound waves. True hearing involves not only receiving the sounds but processing the content of the message, giving it serious consideration, and deciding what course of action should be taken in response to what was heard. In other words, whoever has ears to hear, let him really hear.

A WIDE ANGLE VIEW

1 Recount a story from your life when someone heard the words you spoke but did not really "hear" you.

What kept this person from really hearing you?

A BIBLICAL PORTRAIT

Read 2 Timothy 4:1–5

2 The apostle Paul says people will turn away from hearing the truth and turn their ears toward those who are saying what they want to hear. What are some of the false or unhealthy messages people in our generation are turning their ears to hear?

3 This passage says that many people will plug their ears when it comes to "sound doctrine." When Paul talks about sound doctrine he means the core truth of the Christian faith. What central truths of the Christian faith do people need to hear today?

SHARPENING THE FOCUS

Read Snapshot "Hearing God Speak Through the Bible"

HEARING GOD SPEAK THROUGH THE BIBLE

God's primary way of speaking to His people is through His Word, the Bible. The essence of Christianity is that you have a relationship with God, and what is a relationship without communication?

Years ago when I was involved in youth and college ministry I knew a number of students who were dating people who went to colleges in other states. After a time I could sense when they were getting discouraged because they hadn't seen their boyfriends or girlfriends for a while.

One night a young woman came to a youth meeting with an air of excitement. Obviously, something wonderful had recently happened. I said, "What happened to you?" And she said, "I just talked with my boyfriend." That one talk changed her whole disposition. She had communicated with someone she loved and it changed her whole outlook on life.

The same is true of followers of Christ. People who read the Word regularly and meet with God consistently stand out in a crowd. They hear God speak to their hearts on a daily basis, and it shows! They are so current, vital, and fresh. It's like they just got off the phone with Him.

On the other hand, those who never, or rarely, meet with God and hear Him speak through His Word have a whole different disposition. Their life is stagnant; their outlook depressing. What is the difference between these two groups of people? Some have ears to hear and some don't!

4 Describe a time when God spoke clearly to your heart and life through reading His Word.

5 What is your level of commitment for studying God's Word at this time of your life?

If you want to deepen your commitment in this area of your life, ask others in the group to help you stick to a regular pattern of Bible reading and study.

Read Snapshot "Hearing God Speak Through Preaching and Teaching"

HEARING GOD SPEAK THROUGH PREACHING AND TEACHING

God says in His Word that something supernatural happens when we meet together. Whether we meet on Sundays or Wednesdays, with a large group in a church building or in small groups in a home, God is ready to speak to His people and He wants us to have ears that hear.

This is why it is such a serious responsibility to be a teacher of God's Word. As a matter of fact, in the book of James we read, "Not many of you should presume to be teachers, my brothers, because you know that we who teach will be judged more strictly" (3:1). It is important for teachers of God's Word to make time for enough solitude, submission, and study of the Bible so that God can speak through their words. If a preacher or teacher is living an impure life, God will often not communicate His words, thoughts, and messages through them.

---

6 Describe a time God spoke clearly to you through a sermon, group Bible study, or some other form of teaching.

7

If we are going to hear God speak to us when His Word is taught, we need to learn how to prepare our hearts and remove the obstacles that might keep us from hearing. What are some of the practical things we can do to remove obstacles and prepare our hearts to hear God speak?

Read Snapshot "Hearing God Speak Through the Holy Spirit"

HEARING GOD SPEAK THROUGH THE HOLY SPIRIT

God speaks to us through His Holy Spirit. This means of hearing God's voice is a little less objective and requires a little more maturity, but as you grow up in Christ God will begin to speak to you directly through His Spirit. In Matthew 10: 27 we read, "What I tell you in the dark, speak in the daylight; what is whispered in your ear, proclaim from the roofs." I love that verse. It's sort of a shaded reference to God speaking to His children directly, rather mysteriously, through His Holy Spirit. This is not a reference to hearing an audible voice. It is about God speaking gently to your heart through the voice of His Spirit. When we quiet our hearts and listen, God gives us soft promptings.

Sometimes you might get a strong sense that you need to call somebody to encourage them or to ask how they are doing. After following up on this prompting, you discover that they really needed what you had to say to them. Other times, God's Spirit calls you to confession through a clear sense of conviction regarding the sin in your life. Sometimes God's Spirit speaks to simply remind you that you matter to God, that you are loved, that you are precious in His sight. Whatever the message, it is important to keep your ears and heart open to the voice of the Spirit.

May I give one little hint on learning to hear God speak in this way? You probably won't receive these promptings unless you learn something about solitude. If you're rushing about, you'll probably never get a prompting. But if you quiet your heart from time to time, slow down a little bit and get off the treadmill, it's amazing what God might say to you through the Holy Spirit. After you make sure the message squares with Scripture, be sure to follow what God says.

8

Tell about a time you sensed God speaking to you gently through the voice of His Spirit.

What was He saying and how did you respond?

Read Snapshot "Hearing God Speak Through Other People"

HEARING GOD SPEAK THROUGH OTHER PEOPLE

In His wisdom, there are times God chooses to route a message to you through a brother or a sister in Christ. The amazing thing about this truth is that it means there are times when God might choose to use you as the route He uses to speak to others!

In the Old Testament, King David was thinking about numbering his troops in order to assess his military. His plans were motivated by pride and a spirit of self-sufficiency. I'm sure the Spirit was whispering to David, "Don't do it. It's an act of pride." But David wasn't listening for the Spirit. So God chose to speak to David through a friend named Joab. The great thing about God using Joab was that he was not a priest or a prophet. As a matter of fact, he was a military man.

In 1 Chronicles 21:3 we find Joab pleading with David. He said, "David, don't do it. It doesn't make any difference if you have one thousand or ten thousand men. God is your strength. David, don't do it." But independent David chose not to listen to the voice of God through his friend. He closed his ears, and the results were disastrous. We can learn from this example of David. When God speaks through another person, we should be ready to hear and respond.

 Recount a time God spoke to you through a fellow follower of Christ.

How did you respond to this message from God?

BEING GOD'S MESSENGER

As you pray, ask God if He has something He wants you to say to someone. If He gives you a word of encouragement, challenge, or love, commit yourself to pass it on to this person.

A COMMITMENT TO HEARING GOD SPEAK THROUGH HIS WORD

If you do not have a specific commitment to studying God's Word on a daily basis, take time to set specific one-month goals in this area of your life.

What portion of the Bible will you study?

_____

What time of the day will you study the Bible?

_____

How much time will you commit on a daily basis?

_____

Where will you be when you do your study?

_____

Who will be praying for you and keeping you accountable?

_____

A NEW
VOICE

REFLECTIONS FROM SESSION 3

1. If you accepted the challenge to speak the truth to someone, how did the person respond? Did he or she really
   "hear" you?
2. If you made a commitment to regular study of the Bible,
   how have you done at keeping this commitment?

THE BIG PICTURE

In recent decades many people have debated the issue of nuclear
power plants. Proponents argue that nuclear energy is the only
viable source of power for the twenty-first century. They say
that it will become increasingly efficient and cost-effective
over time, adding that we have to continue development of
nuclear power plants if we are going to supply the energy
needed in the future.

There are also many people who strongly disagree with the
development of nuclear power as a primary source of energy
for the future. Although they acknowledge the good that
nuclear power can do, they feel the potential danger to the
community is not worth the risk. They see the vast potential
for destruction if even one serious breakdown goes undetected.

The Bible says that the human voice has some striking similari-
ties to nuclear power. Our words can be powerfully positive and
can have life-changing impact on those around us. They can
praise God, encourage others, declare the truth, express love,
and do many other things that are positive and constructive.
Yet at the same time, our words have the potential to do the
damage of a nuclear meltdown in the lives of those around us.
We have the potential to do indescribable damage through
our words.

A WIDE ANGLE VIEW

1

Describe a time someone spoke words that had a powerfully positive or negative impact on you.

Tell about a time you spoke words that had a powerfully positive or negative impact on someone else.

A BIBLICAL PORTRAIT

Read James 3:3–12 _Our family_ *

2

James paints a series of pictures that portray the human tongue and its power to build or destroy. What are these images and what is James trying to communicate through them?

3

In verses 6–8 James has some tough things to say about our words and their impact. If you agree with this harsh assessment, explain why. If you think James is overstating his case, explain why.

Read Snapshot "The Power of the Voice . . . to Destroy"

THE POWER OF THE VOICE . . . TO DESTROY

If we were to commit a physical homicide we would end up in jail, and rightly so. There are civil laws against murder. But verbal homicide is legal. There are no laws to keep people from cutting into a person's heart with words from a razor-sharp tongue.

We have all been victims of such verbal attacks, and we have all been perpetrators. These attacks take place in master bedrooms, in family rooms, on job sites, in offices and conference rooms, in locker rooms, across back fences, and in churches. They seem to happen everywhere. When we are not careful, we can find our words filled with venom, our tongues sharp as a sword, and our voices weapons of destruction.

4

There is an old saying, "Sticks and stones can break my bones, but words will never hurt me." As an adult looking back on your life experience, how do you respond to this saying?

5

We have all been guilty of striking out at others with our words. Sometimes our attacks are accidental or simply a reflexive response to our own pain. At other times the damage is intentional and thought through in advance. If you have a person in your life who you have hurt with your words, what do you need to do to make things right with this person?

How can your group members support you in this commitment and keep you accountable to follow through?

If you can't stop yourself from not inflicting - maybe you shouldn't be trying to correct someone.

Read Snapshot "The Power of the Voice . . . to Build Up"

THE POWER OF THE VOICE . . . TO BUILD UP

Not only do we know the pain and sting of hurtful words, but we have all experienced the exhilaration and euphoria of having someone use their voice constructively to build us up and affirm us. The truth is, our voice can do unbelievable amounts of good. Through it, we have the power to bring joy to the life of others.

Did you know that most pastors and Christian leaders who leave the ministry do so because of discouragement? What they need is people who will build them up and affirm them. How many marriages break down because communication ceases? Many spouses do not live with a commitment to be encouragers. How many partnerships in businesses disintegrate when people stop affirming each other? How many friendships would find new life if we committed ourselves to use our words to build each other up?

You have the equivalent of nuclear power in your voice if you learn to use it constructively. First Thessalonians 5:11 says, "Encourage one another and build each other up." This should become our life motto!

6

Tell your group about a person in your life who has consistently used their words to encourage and build you up. How has this person impacted your life?

7

Who is one person you need to encourage and build up with your words? What can you do in the coming days to use your voice to affirm that person and lift him or her up?

Doug
Lisa
Carpenter

Let God's word
dwell in us
what we choose to
Richly
our minds with
intimately with his
will

as a christian!
It's a choice to
build someone up as
tear them down

Read Snapshot "The Power of the Voice . . . to Worship God"

THE POWER OF THE VOICE . . . TO WORSHIP GOD

If you want to use your voice constructively, there's even a higher plane. You can use it to worship God. In the morning when the sun is rising, lift up your voice and sing, "Oh Lord, our Lord, how majestic is Your Name in all the earth." Throughout the day let your voice sing of God's goodness. God's Word says that He loves to hear the praises of His children.

It is a beautiful thing to use your voice to affirm the great truths of the faith and your appreciation for His handiwork. When you see a beautiful sunset, a bird flying high above, or something in creation that jumps out and grabs your attention, tell God, "You are the Creator, and I affirm the fact that You did an outstanding job." He appreciates those who notice the beauty of all He has made.

God also longs for our statements of affection. To say, "Lord, I love you because You first loved me" warms the heart of God.

8

Name a song that really helps you express worship to God. What is it in this song that helps you communicate your praise and love?

9

Take time as a group to express your love for God. Simply tell each other why you love the Lord and what He means to you. If your group enjoys singing together, worship Him through song for a few moments.

PUTTING YOURSELF IN THE PICTURE

TOOLS FOR CONTROLLING THE TONGUE

Take time in the coming days to develop one or more of the following skills in relationship to your words:

- Proverbs 10:19 says, "He who holds his tongue is wise." The more you say, the higher the probability that you will say something you will regret. When in doubt, it's best to keep quiet.
- Proverbs 17:28 says, "Even a fool is thought wise if he keeps silent, and discerning if he holds his tongue." If you want to really impress somebody and convince them you are wise, learn to practice silence. You don't have to enter into every conversation. Sometimes a few words are a few too many.

- Proverbs 15:1 gives us another helpful hint. It says to let your words be gentle. Mature discussions among well-adjusted people explode when the volume increases. We have all seen it happen. A conversation starts with soft words and reasonable concerns expressed. As the volume increases, reason seems to decrease. By the time people are yelling, reason has left the room! If you have to go into a delicate situation, Scripture says, speak gently.

- You can tell what's really going on in a person's heart by listening to what comes out of their mouth. If you observe a person over a period of time who has a dirty mouth, you can be pretty safe in concluding that they have a dirty heart. Hateful words may mean a hateful heart. Pure words likely indicate a pure heart. And if someone uses encouraging words, they most likely have a heart that's overflowing with the love of Jesus Christ. We need to listen to what comes out of our mouths to gain some insight into the areas which God wants to change in our own lives.

Prov. 17:21

Vanessa — pray for her to be wise kind & gentle to the kids not being wise - where are her boundaries
Rob → filled w/ Spirit
Rob & Leslie — help w/ patience to deal w/ stress with
Pray for her parents (mom)   living quarters
living situation   dad

Kathy — for son Jeremy — Cassidy — "bond w/   Greensborough
Va Beach   to feel that   Grace —
there is a bond there   develop a good
relationship w/
Kathy   mini Ben — still not sure what fiancé Steve
he wants from life - give him
direction & help
Praise — Marshall looks great
pray for her job — strength - ears to
hear what God
wants her to hear

41

NEW HANDS

REFLECTIONS FROM SESSION 4

1. If you made an effort to practice the discipline of silence by holding your tongue, how did it go? What makes being quiet so challenging?
2. If you have made a commitment to try and speak more gently, how has this impacted your relationships?

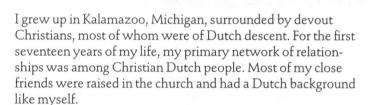

THE BIG PICTURE

I grew up in Kalamazoo, Michigan, surrounded by devout Christians, most of whom were of Dutch descent. For the first seventeen years of my life, my primary network of relationships was among Christian Dutch people. Most of my close friends were raised in the church and had a Dutch background like myself.

As I was growing up, I spent time in the homes of my friends around Kalamazoo, Holland, and Grand Rapids, Michigan. Over time I began to notice that in almost every one of my friends' homes was the same picture. Most often the picture was on the kitchen wall, but sometimes it was on a dining-room wall. It got so that when I was in the home of a new friend, I would actually look for this picture and would wonder where it might be located in their home.

Those who are curious are probably wondering what the picture was. You might even be guessing right now. Well, let me take away the suspense. It was a picture of praying hands. Have you ever seen it? Tan, rugged, weather-beaten, calloused hands pointing reverently heavenward. For the Dutch people in the community where I was raised, that picture was worth a thousand words. You see, the Dutch people I knew were hard-working, reverent, God-fearing people. It was as though that picture was the unofficial symbol of their faith. Their reverence for God and their dependency on Him was portrayed in those praying hands.

1 Why do you think so many people find such deep meaning in a picture of praying hands?

A BIBLICAL PORTRAIT

Read Proverbs 6:16–17; Ecclesiastes 10:18; Matthew 5:30

2 These passages give us warnings about our hands. What warnings do you hear when you read these passages?

How would you translate these warnings into today's language?

Read Matthew 8:1–4; Luke 18:15–17

3

Through His ministry, Jesus often reached out and touched people with His hands. Why do you think this was so important to Jesus?

How is this an example to us as we interact with others?

SHARPENING THE FOCUS

Read Snapshot "Uplifted Hands"

UPLIFTED HANDS

Picture two hands uplifted toward heaven. Hands reaching high toward the sky. The hands are open. They're reaching. They're stretching. They might be trembling a little bit, but you sense that there is an air of expectancy about them. There seems to be a curious tension between fearfulness and trust. As you look at that picture, ask yourself this question: What does it symbolize?

I see at least three distinct messages in this picture. First, hands lifted heavenward can symbolize somebody reaching up, crying out for salvation. You see, every person who becomes a follower of Christ comes to the point where they have to lift up their hands and receive God's gracious gift of salvation through Jesus Christ. There is no other way.

Second, lifted hands can also symbolize intense prayer. We all face times when we realize our resources, abilities, and strength just won't get the job done. With hands stretching heavenward we cry out to God in prayer and discover His power can carry us through.

Third, this picture of lifted hands can also symbolize worship. All through the Bible we read of people lifting their hands in worship. Hands lifted can be a picture of lifting our hearts, our lives, our praise, our worship up toward our Maker.

4

What are some of the things that have happened in your life that led up to you finally lifting your hands to heaven and calling out to God for forgiveness of sins?

5

What one need in your life right now do you need to lift to God in prayer?

6

What different body postures help you express worship to God (standing, kneeling, folding hands, lifting hands, bowing your head . . .)?

Why does expressing your worship physically help you express what is in your heart?

Read Snapshot "Hand in Hand"

HAND IN HAND

Now paint another picture. Picture a person firmly grasping the hand of someone they know. A neighbor stretches out his hand and another grasps it with both hands. Or picture two business partners closing a deal with a firm handshake. Or you might envision a small group of Christians praying with their hands joined together.

In Galatians 2:9 Paul makes a reference to Christians extending the right hand of fellowship to other believers. This picture symbolizes brotherhood and sisterhood. It reminds us that we are part of the family of God through Jesus Christ. It also encourages us to warmly extend the invitation of community to someone who is seeking Christ.

---

7 What are some practical ways you can extend your hand to other believers in an effort to build Christian community?

What is one specific thing you can do in the coming week to reach a hand out to another follower of Christ?

8 What is one practical way your small group can extend a hand of Christian care to a brother or sister in need?

Read Snapshot "Hands on the Plow"

HANDS ON THE PLOW

You may have never seen a horse-drawn plow, but you have probably seen pictures. The hands are calloused, the wood of the plow handles worn smooth from years of use. The hands seem to fit on the plow handles naturally, reflecting the days, months, and years of work they have done together.

This picture comes from the Bible. In Luke 9:62 Jesus says, "No one who puts his hand to the plow and looks back is fit for service in the kingdom of God." These words are not a reference to ordinary vocational labor; they remind us that every follower of Christ is called to put their hands on a kingdom plow. We are to discover our special calling, the ministry God called us to do, and then start doing this work for God's glory. Every follower of Christ has the great privilege of serving God by taking the plow and ministering in Jesus' name.

9

Describe a ministry you have been involved in and how this ministry was or is an expression of your love for God.

10

What is one area of ministry you have always desired to participate in but have never pursued?

What can you do to put your hands to the plow and become involved in this area of ministry?

Lifting Your Hands in Prayer

Identify three specific needs in your life or the lives of those close to you. Commit yourself to lift your hands and heart in prayer for these needs every day until your small group meets again. If these are needs you feel comfortable communicating to others, ask one of your small group members to join you in lifting these needs to God in prayer.

A Commitment to Take the Plow

If you are not presently serving God through some kind of ministry, take at least one of the following steps to help you discover where God might be calling you to serve:

- Pray for the prompting and leading of the Holy Spirit.
- Take a class on spiritual gifts and ministry to help you discover how God has gifted and made you for ministry. If your church does not offer a class like this, you may want to talk with a church leader about looking into the curriculum called "Network: Understanding God's Design for You in the Church." This curriculum is used at Willow Creek and in many other churches across the country.
- Seek counsel from other Christians you respect. Ask them where they might see you fitting into ministry in your church or community.
- Meet with a pastor or church leader and ask for their prayers, wisdom, and support as you seek to discover where you might commit yourself to minister.

A NEW SPINE

REFLECTIONS FROM SESSION 5

1. What are some of the answers to prayers you have seen in the past few weeks?
2. If you have been investigating becoming involved in some area of ministry, what progress have you made?

THE BIG PICTURE

I want to share an experience from my own life that comes from a bleak moment of my teenage years. I would say that it rates as one of the worst moments of my life. In Kalamazoo, Michigan, there was a drive-in restaurant where kids would hang out on Friday and Saturday nights. It was the highlight of our week. We would save up money all week long so we could afford to burn a tank or two of gas driving around and showing off our cars on the weekend evenings. That was the totality of our social experience, and so we really went for it.

One night, when I was a junior in high school, I spent the whole evening driving around and hanging out with my friends. On my way home I was alone in the car and, as I was getting ready to make a left-hand turn onto the expressway, I saw another car coming from the other direction. I had seen this car driving around earlier in the evening and knew it was filled with seven or eight teenagers. The minute I saw them making the turn in front of me, I knew they were driving way too fast. Right before my eyes the car jumped the median and slammed head-on into the guardrail. I wasn't more than a hundred feet from the accident.

In that moment I saw the windshield explode as two of the students went through it. The doors swung open and bodies came flying out. It was a devastating accident. I was the only person there not involved in the crash and my reaction was one of stark terror. I have a thing about violence and blood; I just can't handle them. I don't go to any movies where there's a lot of bloodshed. I'm not a very strong person when it comes to seeing people suffer.

I knew the inside of that car was going to be a disaster. I also knew the right thing to do was to stop. But in just a fraction of a second, I faced a moment of truth when I had to decide what I was going to do. Was I going to stop and offer assistance or was I going to keep driving down the expressway? In that fraction of a second, all I could think of was how awful it would be to come face-to-face with all of those broken and bloody bodies. I was so frightened and upset by what I had already seen that I did not know what to do. A voice inside me was crying out, "Just keep driving." Another voice was saying, "You better stop." I hate to admit it, but I caved in. I drove right around the accident and onto the highway.

When I got to the next exit, I called for an ambulance. But let me tell you, if you could have looked inside my heart for some time following this event, you would have seen an element of self-hatred so deep that it would defy description. Every time I saw a picture on the front page of the local newspaper about any car accident, I got flashbacks. A voice cut into my heart, "You are a spineless coward." I started to tell myself that if I was ever in a situation like that again, I'd act differently. I even confessed to the Lord, "Oh Lord, I sinned when I failed to stop and help those kids." Over time I experienced His forgiveness in the matter, but it still didn't completely remove the scar.

A couple of years later, I was driving a truck through Indiana on the way to Chicago to pick up a load of produce. Late in the afternoon I saw a little Toyota run off the road and into the field at a high rate of speed. It started flipping end over end. Immediately I had another one of those moments of truth. I looked and I saw the three cars in front of me drive right by the accident and it brought a vivid flashback to my mind.

I remember thinking that whoever is in that car was going to be all torn up. I also realized that I could not live with myself if I didn't stop. I made my decision, by God's grace, and in the fraction of a second, I locked up all the wheels on that truck and skidded off the side of the road.

I knew that if I thought about it for half a second, I might cave in again. Quickly, I threw the truck door open and ran as fast as I could to the car. Every single step was a choice, a decision of my will. I knew that whatever I would find out there was going to be awful and that I would probably get sick to my stomach before this was over. But I also remembered what it felt like to cave in, and I was not going to live through that again. Sure enough, when I got to the accident the driver was in terrible condition. She was unconscious and she was a mess. I found an overcoat that had fallen out of the trunk and I put it over her and just sat with her out in that field until an ambulance arrived and the medics loaded her up.

I was trembling as I drove the rest of the way to Chicago. But way down deep there was something inside of me that said, "You did the right thing. You learned a lesson. You learned something about courage."

A WIDE ANGLE VIEW

1 What is one act of courage you have witnessed in your lifetime?

A BIBLICAL PORTRAIT

Read Snapshot "A Story of Courage"

A STORY OF COURAGE

As a teenage counselor at a Bible camp I remember being chosen to tell the story of David and Goliath to a group of kids from Chicago who had no biblical background. To my amazement, they had never heard this classic Bible story.

I can remember telling the story and watching those kids' eyes. I told them about a little boy named David who was the youngest child in a family of lots of boys. I told them how David was sent to check up on his brothers and bring them some food. I painted a picture of a ten-foot-tall monster of a man named Goliath, who wore armor like a military tank.

I explained that even though David's older brothers were soldiers, they were afraid of Goliath. No one would go out and fight against him. But then little David said that he would fight the giant. I told them about David trying on the king's armor but finally deciding to go with the one weapon he knew, a sling and stone. I painted a picture of David approaching Goliath as the giant laughed at him and called him a dog. Then I told them how little, courageous David shot one stone at full force and how it hit Goliath right in the forehead, crushing through his skull and knocking him down. Finally, I described how David stood with his foot on the neck of Goliath as all the people of Israel shouted and praised God.

You should have seen those little campers' eyes. They were filled with amazement. The human spirit responds to stories of courage. It evokes something in us that we aspire toward. David's name, even today, is synonymous with courage. As you read this classic biblical story of courage, try to hear it for the first time even if you have heard it many times before.

Read 1 Samuel 17:20–51

2 How did David show courage in *one* of the following ways:

- In the presence of his brothers
- Before the King of Israel
- Standing before Goliath
- Before his God

3 Respond to this statement: David's courage, greatness, and faith were formed during the years he committed himself to do the thankless job of shepherding. David learned courage when no one was watching, and he became great by doing a common and thankless job with excellence. David was a man of courage long before he met Goliath.

What are some of your daily commitments and responsibilities that teach you courage?

SHARPENING THE FOCUS

Read Snapshot, "Believe the Promises of God"

BELIEVE THE PROMISES OF GOD

It takes incredible courage to believe the promises of God! Every human being needs to face and deal with four essential truths. First, we are all moral failures. We have all sinned and come short of God's standards. Second, we will stand before a holy God who doesn't have even a shadow of sin in His character. Third, we can't clean up our act on our own. We can't change our condition no matter how hard we might try. We will stand condemned before a holy God. Fourth, unless we trust in Jesus Christ, we are lost. His death on the cross is our only hope of forgiveness. He took our punishment and judgment so we could be free.

4 We live in a world that is often hostile to the message of Christ and antagonistic to followers of Christ who really stand up for their faith. Choose *one* of the places below and describe the kind of courage it takes to stand for your Christian faith:

- In the marketplace
- In your neighborhood
- Among family members who don't believe in Christ
- In the political arena
- Around seekers you meet through various social contacts

5 What are some of the sacrifices and lifestyle changes you have made since becoming a follower of Christ?

How have these changes and sacrifices demanded courage?

6 What is one commitment you know God wants you to make, but that you have been resisting?

What is it going to take for you to have the courage to make this commitment?

Read Snapshot "Living Out the Principles of God"

LIVING OUT THE PRINCIPLES OF GOD

Do you know what real backbone is? It's living as a fully devoted follower of Christ in a world that is unsympathetic to Christian values. This means learning to live out God's principles even when it hurts. One call of God on the life of every Christian is to tell others about the love of Jesus. This does not have to be done in an abrasive and confrontational manner, but it must be done. All Christ followers must learn how to communicate the message of Christ in a way that fits their temperament and makeup. Jesus said to His followers, "I send you out as sheep among wolves," and He meant it. Those who hide their true identity and try to live in two different worlds will cave in. It takes real courage to communicate the message of Jesus in our day and age. Do you have the spine for it?

7

Tell about a time you had the courage to express your faith in some way and stand up as a Christian.

What gave you courage and boldness in this situation?

8

Describe a time you knew you should communicate your faith, but something kept you from doing it.

What was it that stood in the way of you communicating your love for Jesus in this situation?

9

What have you discovered that helps you communicate your faith with courage and clarity?

PUTTING YOURSELF IN THE PICTURE

1. Identify one lifestyle change or commitment you believe God wants you to make. If you are lacking the courage to face this challenge, pray for the Holy Spirit to fill your heart with courage and begin acting on God's prompting in this area of your life.

2. It is essential for every follower of Christ to learn how they can freely and naturally communicate the message of salvation in Jesus Christ. Commit yourself to learning how to communicate your faith with clarity and courage. If your church does not offer a class on evangelism, talk with a pastor or church leader about starting one. You may want to consider reviewing the "Becoming a Contagious Christian" program. This curriculum gives practical training in evangelism that helps participants discover a style of evangelism that fits them.

Leader's Notes

Leading a Bible discussion—especially for the first time—can make you feel both nervous and excited. If you are nervous, realize that you are in good company. Many biblical leaders, such as Moses, Joshua, and the apostle Paul, felt nervous and inadequate to lead others (see, for example, 1 Cor. 2:3). Yet God's grace was sufficient for them, just as it will be for you.

Some excitement is also natural. Your leadership is a gift to the others in the group. Keep in mind, however, that other group members also share responsibility for the group. Your role is simply to stimulate discussion by asking questions and encouraging people to respond. The suggestions listed below can help you to be an effective leader.

Preparing to Lead

1. Ask God to help you understand and apply the passage to your own life. Unless that happens, you will not be prepared to lead others.
2. Carefully work through each question in the study guide. Meditate and reflect on the passage as you formulate your answers.
3. Familiarize yourself with theLeader's Notes for each session. These will help you understand the purpose of the session and will provide valuable information about the questions in the session. The Leader's Notes are not intended to be read to the group. These notes are primarily for your use as a group leader and for your preparation. However, when you find a section that relates well to your group, you may want to read a brief portion or encourage them to read this section at another time.
4. Pray for the various members of the group. Ask God to use these sessions to make you better disciples of Jesus Christ.
5. Before the first session, make sure each person has a study guide. Encourage them to prepare beforehand for each session.

LEADING THE SESSION

1. Begin the session on time. If people realize that the session begins on schedule, they will work harder to arrive on time.
2. At the beginning of your first time together, explain that these sessions are designed to be discussions, not lectures. Encourage everyone to participate, but realize some may be hesitant to speak during the first few sessions.
3. Don't be afraid of silence. People in the group may need time to think before responding.
4. Avoid answering your own questions. If necessary, rephrase a question until it is clearly understood. Even an eager group will quickly become passive and silent if they think the leader will do most of the talking.
5. Encourage more than one answer to each question. Ask, "What do the rest of you think?" or "Anyone else?" until several people have had a chance to respond.
6. Try to be affirming whenever possible. Let people know you appreciate their insights into the passage.
7. Never reject an answer. If it is clearly wrong, ask, "Which verse led you to that conclusion?" Or let the group handle the problem by asking them what they think about the question.
8. Avoid going off on tangents. If people wander off course, gently bring them back to the passage being considered.
9. Conclude your time together with conversational prayer. Ask God to help you apply those things that you learned in the session.
10. End on time. This will be easier if you control the pace of the discussion by not spending too much time on some questions or too little on others.

We encourage all small group leaders to use *Leading Life-Changing Small Groups* (Zondervan) by Bill Donahue and the Willow Creek Small Group Team while leading their group. Developed and used by Willow Creek Community Church, this guide is an excellent resource for training and equipping followers of Christ to effectively lead small groups. It includes valuable information on how to utilize fun and creative relationship-building exercises for your group; how to plan your meeting; how to share the leadership load by identifying, developing, and working with an "apprentice leader"; and how to find creative ways to do group prayer. In addition, the book includes material and tips on handling potential conflicts and difficult personalities, forming group covenants, inviting new members, improving listening skills, studying the Bible, and much more. Using *Leading Life-Changing Small Groups* will help you create a group that members love to be a part of.

Now let's discuss the different elements of this small group study guide and how to use them for the session portion of your group meeting.

THE BIG PICTURE

Each session will begin with a short story or overview of the lesson theme. This is called "The Big Picture" because it introduces the central theme of the session. You will need to read this section as a group or have group members read it on their own before discussion begins. Here are three ways you can approach this section of the small group session:

- As the group leader, read this section out loud for the whole group and then move into the questions in the next section, "A Wide Angle View." (You might read the first week, but then use the other two options below to encourage group involvement.)
- Ask a group member to volunteer to read this section for the group. This allows another group member to participate. It is best to ask someone in advance to give them time to read over the section before reading it to the group. It is also good to ask someone to volunteer, and not to assign this task. Some people do not feel comfortable reading in front of a group. After a group member has read this section out loud, move into the discussion questions.
- Allow time at the beginning of the session for each person to read this section silently. If you do this, be sure to allow enough time for everyone to finish reading so they can think about what they've read and be ready for meaningful discussion.

A WIDE ANGLE VIEW

This section includes one or more questions that move the group into a general discussion of the session topic. These questions are designed to help group members begin discussing the topic in an open and honest manner. Once the topic of the lesson has been established, move on to the Bible passage for the session.

A BIBLICAL PORTRAIT

This portion of the session includes a Scripture reading and one or more questions that help group members see how the theme of the session is rooted and based in biblical teaching. The Scripture reading can be handled just like "The Big Picture" section: You can read it for the group, have a group member read it, or allow time for silent reading. Make sure everyone has a Bible or that you have Bibles available for those who need them. Once you have read the passage, ask the question(s) in this section so that group members can dig into the truth of the Bible.

SHARPENING THE FOCUS

The majority of the discussion questions for the session are in this section. These questions are practical and help group members apply biblical teaching to their daily lives.

SNAPSHOTS

The "Snapshots" in each session help prepare group members for discussion. These anecdotes give additional insight to the topic being discussed. Each "Snapshot" should be read at a designated point in the session. This is clearly marked in the session as well as in the Leader's Notes. Again, follow the same format as you do with "The Big Picture" section and the "Biblical Portrait" section: Either you read the anecdote, have a group member volunteer to read, or provide time for silent reading. However you approach this section, you will find these anecdotes very helpful in triggering lively dialogue and moving discussion in a meaningful direction.

PUTTING YOURSELF IN THE PICTURE

Here's where you roll up your sleeves and put the truth into action. This portion is very practical and action-oriented. At the end of each session there will be suggestions for one or two ways group members can put what they've just learned into practice. Review the action goals at the end of each session and challenge group members to work on one or more of them in the coming week.

You will find follow-up questions for the "Putting Yourself in the Picture" section at the beginning of the next week's session. Starting with the second week, there will be time set aside at the beginning of the session to look back and talk about how you have tried to apply God's Word in your life since your last time together.

PRAYER

You will want to open and close your small group with a time of prayer. Occasionally, there will be specific direction within a session for how you can do this. Most of the time, however, you will need to decide the best place to stop and pray. You may want to pray or have a group member volunteer to begin the lesson with a prayer. Or you might want to read "The Big Picture" and discuss the "Wide Angle View" questions before opening in prayer. In some cases, it might be best to open in prayer after you have read the Bible passage. You need to decide where you feel an opening prayer best fits for your group.

When opening in prayer, think in terms of the session theme and pray for group members (including yourself) to be responsive to the truth of Scripture and the working of the Holy Spirit. If you have seekers in your group (people investigating Christianity but not yet believers), be sensitive to your expectations for group prayer. Seekers may not yet be ready to take part in group prayer.

Be sure to close your group with a time of prayer as well. One option is for you to pray for the entire group. Or you might allow time for group members to offer audible prayers that others can agree with in their hearts. Another approach would be to allow a time of silence for one-on-one prayers with God and then to close this time with a simple "Amen."

A NEW HEART
Ezekiel 11:17–21; 36:24–28

INTRODUCTION

There is absolutely no limit to what God can do with soft-hearted women or men. He can pour His love into their hearts because He knows it will be received and not spurned. He can send His blessing because He knows it will lead to deep worship. He can give direction and guidance because He knows it will be followed. He can give opportunities for effectiveness in the kingdom because He knows they will be treasured. He can give ideas and creative bursts of inspiration because He knows they will be appreciated and used for His glory. This session exposes the truth that hard-hearted people need to receive new hearts from God. Then, once we have our new hearts, we need to continually soften them so that we are responsive to God moment by moment and day by day.

THE BIG PICTURE

Take time to read this introduction with the group. There are suggestions for how this can be done in the beginning of this leader's section.

A BIBLICAL PORTRAIT

Read Ezekiel 11:17–21; 36:24–28

Questions Two & Three Ezekiel realized that his people needed a whole new heart; the old one had been irreparably damaged and diseased. That's why in Ezekiel 36:26, God says through the prophet, "I will remove from you your heart of stone and give you a heart of flesh." The old stone heart that was unresponsive to God and insensitive to others would be replaced by a new heart of flesh that was soft, responsive to God, and sensitive to others. What this means for us today is that we need more than a few subtle modifications on the inside; we need complete transformation. We don't need heart repair; we need a transplant. Jesus told Nicodemus in John 3, "You don't need modification; you need to be born again. You need a whole new you. A whole new heart."

SHARPENING THE FOCUS

Read Snapshot "A Hard Heart" before Question 4

Questions Four & Five If you're hard-hearted toward God, to some degree you will be hard-hearted toward people. There are many biblical examples of this, and the one that sticks out in my mind is King Herod. Herod was paranoid because he heard that another king had been born who was called Jesus. He was so threatened by Jesus' birth that he sent the Roman soldiers into Bethlehem to murder *all* the baby boys. Can you imagine? That's a hard-hearted man!

There are also modern-day examples, obvious atrocities we have all heard about on the news and read about in the papers. We have all had our stomachs sickened by accounts of sexual abuse in day-care centers. How can anyone abuse a one- or two-year-old baby? We hear of senseless beatings, rapes, and murders and we realize that we live in a hard-hearted world.

However, before we focus on the worst examples, let's not forget the everyday emotional atrocities we inflict on each other. We launch verbal missiles at each other with regularity and deadly accuracy. We send cold stares that chill the hearts of others and turn our backs on those we could help but refuse to because of our selfishness. We need to recognize the slander, the nicknames, the potshots, and the subtle jabs that decimate a brother or a sister bit by bit. Our unwillingness to forgive is also a sign of hard-heartedness. And even withholding desperately needed encouragement shows our heart is not as tender as it should be.

Read Snapshot "A New Heart" before Question 6

Questions Six & Seven When you see the condition of your heart before God, you will say, "I know my heart is sick, unresponsive to God, and insensitive to others." You will pray, "Lord, Jesus died on the cross and paid the price for my sin. He has allowed me to have a new heart. Please make it so in my life." When this happens, you will get a new, soft heart. Your attitudes will begin to change, first toward God and then toward others.

That's why it's dangerous for hard-hearted people to hang around with true followers of Christ. True believers know God's Word, use the Word, live the Word, share the Word. Hard-hearted people find out after awhile that if they hang around with true Christians they're going to get pierced with the truth.

Read Snapshot "A Soft Heart" before Question 8

Questions Eight & Nine People with new, softened hearts melt their way into each other's lives. They become bound together as brothers and sisters with cords that can't be broken. They look for ways to express their love and lift each other's burdens. They sense when someone is wandering off the path and ask, "What can I do to help you get on the right path? How can I support you and pray for you?" They sense when someone is exhausted and under pressure or frightened or insecure, and they minister to that person. With new, soft hearts, our love for God and others grows deeper every day.

PUTTING YOURSELF IN THE PICTURE

Tell group members you will be providing time at the beginning of the next meeting for them to discuss how they have put their faith into practice. Let them tell their stories. However, don't limit their interaction to the two options provided. They may have put themselves into the picture in some other way as a result of your study. Allow for honest and open communication.

Also, be clear that there will not be any kind of a "test" or forced reporting. All you are going to do is allow time for people to volunteer to talk about how they have applied what they learned in your last study. Some group members will feel pressured if they think you are going to make everyone provide a "report." You don't want anyone to skip the next group because they are afraid of having to say they did not follow up on what they learned from the prior session. Focus instead on providing a place for honest communication without creating pressure or fear of being embarrassed.

Every session from this point on will open with a look back at the "Putting Yourself in the Picture" section of the previous session.

A NEW MIND

Romans 12:1–3

INTRODUCTION

Second Corinthians 5:17 says, "Therefore, if anyone is in Christ, he is a new creation; the old has gone, the new has come!" This transformation starts with the heart. When we realize that we have the disease of hard-heartedness, we must look to God for the cure. Spiritual surgery that pierces us with God's truth is necessary so that we can receive a new heart.

Once we have a new heart we realize this is only the start of a process of transformation that will last a lifetime. Along with needing a new heart, the Scriptures teach us that we need a transformed mind as well. God wants us to have a mind that is razor sharp, discerning, and quick to respond to His will. However, too often we can be dull-minded, allowing the razor's edge of our mind to become a ragged edge. In this session we will focus on how we can allow God to transform our minds daily so that we are always living with the razor's edge when it comes to our thinking.

THE BIG PICTURE

Take time to read this introduction with the group. There are suggestions for how this can be done in the beginning of this leader's section.

A WIDE ANGLE VIEW

Question One In the "Big Picture" section of this session is an example of mental tenacity. Here are two more examples of this essential element of a transformed mind.

If you have ever played baseball or if you know much about the sport, you know that one of the most difficult things to do is to learn to hit a curveball. Here's what happens: The pitcher winds up and throws a little projectile seventy to eighty miles an hour straight at the batter's body. What do you usually do when you see something flying straight at your body with blurring speed? You jump back! A well-thrown curveball gets to about six to eight feet from the batter's body before breaking on a very sharp angle right over the center of the plate.

While you're jumping back out of the box, the ball curves right over the plate, the umpire calls strike, and you look like a fool. The only way to hit a curveball is to stay in the box, even when everything inside of you cries out to jump back. You must have the mental tenacity to stay in the box and swing away. Without this commitment and mental toughness, you will never hit a curveball.

Or how about golf? When making a difficult putt, a golfer takes into account the break of the green. Sometimes this means hitting a putt forty-five degrees away from the hole, believing the break of the green will bring it back. Even though you want to putt straight at the hole, you have to force yourself to play the break. This takes commitment and mental tenacity.

A BIBLICAL PORTRAIT

Read Romans 12:1–3

Questions Two & Three The Bible tells us that our old minds were limited in their ability to ascertain spiritual truth. This is why so many followers of Christ say things like, "Before I gave my heart to Christ, I heard all the words about Christianity, but they did not make sense. I heard people talk about Jesus as the Savior, but I never understood how this related to me. I heard people say I needed to have a personal relationship with Jesus in order to have eternal life, but I had no idea what it meant." Second Corinthians 4:4 says, "The god of this age has blinded the minds of unbelievers, so that they cannot see the light of the gospel of the glory of Christ, who is the image of God." You see, the war for souls is fought on the battlefield of the mind. Satan tries to blind our minds so we don't see our need for a Savior and the truth of God. That's the problem with the old mind; it can't understand the message of Jesus Christ.

Once you are a follower of Christ, you begin to see things more clearly. Not only do you identify the strategies of the enemy, but you also see the patterns of this world that are in opposition to God. God's will grows more and more clear and you are able to order your life after the patterns of God's will rather than after the ways of the world.

SHARPENING THE FOCUS

Read Snapshot "The Razor's Edge" before Question 4

Questions Four & Five Brand-new Christians, as a rule, are simply overwhelmed by the implications of their newly found salvation. They realize they are no longer guilty before God. They have a profound sense that they are forgiven. They often bubble over with joy as they declare, "I have no more fear of death or hell." They say, "Jesus Christ, who used to seem so far away, is now my Savior and my Friend." They are confident that they are going to heaven for all eternity. This razor's edge thinking is something we need to encourage. We all need to learn how to keep this kind of clear thinking, joy, and awe alive in our minds.

Read Snapshot "The Ragged Edge" before Question 6

Questions Six & Seven Some time ago a pastor called me to discuss a decision about taking a leadership position in a church. He said, "I have a great opportunity, but there's only one problem—the church is filled to capacity with seasoned, veteran Christians. Most of them have been Christians for twenty to thirty years." I said, "Okay, what's the problem?" He said, "You know the problem. You know what seasoned, veteran Christians are like. No vision. No love. No joy. No heart for hurting people. No vitality. No creativity. They're dead."

What a heartbreaking statement! Christians, of all people, ought to be filled to overflowing with joy and with the awe of their salvation. Those who have seen God's faithfulness over the years ought to be living with the razor's edge, but too often they are living with the ragged edge.

Read Snapshot "Sharpening the Edge" before Question 8

Questions Eight & Nine If we are going to sharpen the edge of our thinking, we need to continually remember who we are in Christ and what we have as His followers.

What do you have in Christ? Go over the list every day if you must. The basics are what a razor's-edge spiritual life is all about. Never forget that the Bible teaches that the consequences of our sin is death. We deserve death—separation from God forever. But each day we need to remember that we have been saved. We are adopted into the family of God. We are loved. We are filled with the Holy Spirit. Our eternity is secure. We have been equipped with spiritual gifts, have the Word of God, enjoy fellowship in the church, and are surrounded by brothers and sisters in Christ who love us and are like family. Psalm 23 reminds us that goodness and mercy will follow us like a shadow all the days of our life, and on top of that, we will dwell with God forever in eternity.

The major issue of our eternity is settled. When we mope around and live with ragged-edge thinking, we are like millionaires crying over lost pocket change. It's time to sharpen the edge of our thinking so we will see things as they really are.

PUTTING YOURSELF IN THE PICTURE

Challenge group members to take time in the coming week to use part or all of this application section as an opportunity for continued growth.

NEW EARS

2 Timothy 4:1–5

INTRODUCTION

Becoming a new creation in Christ starts with receiving a whole new heart. Everybody has a heart disease called hard-heartedness. To cure this disease, we need to repent of our sins and cry out for Jesus Christ to come into our lives and forgive us from our sins. When we receive a new heart, we also receive a new mind so that we can understand and respond to spiritual truth. The miracle of transformation continues as God gives all believers ears that can hear His voice through His Word, through His Holy Spirit, and through His people.

Before a person gives his life to Christ he has ears, but he can't make sense of God's voice. In Mark 8:18 Jesus said that some people have ears but still can't hear. They can't process spiritual truth. They can hear earthly sounds, but not heavenly communication. This session is about learning to tune our ears in to hear the voice of God as He seeks to speak to us each day. If we have ears to hear, we will learn to hear the voice of God and follow His leading.

THE BIG PICTURE

Take time to read this introduction with the group. There are suggestions for how this can be done in the beginning of this leader's section.

A BIBLICAL PORTRAIT

Read 2 Timothy 4:1–5

Questions Two & Three Second Timothy 4:3 says that some people actually begin to identify teachers or voices that will only "tickle their ears." Some people avoid hearing truth. They surround themselves with sounds, voices, and values that make them feel good. They realize they are shutting out truth, but the truth is too uncomfortable for them to face. It makes them nervous. It bothers them. So they put themselves in situations where they are guaranteed to hear only what they want to hear. We need to identify these "ear-tickling" voices and block them out.

Not only do we need to block out the lies, but we need to tune our ears to hear the truth, even when it is painful. We need to hear certain core truths, and to believe them and pass them on to others. Some of these truths are tough to hear and others are the best news in human history. Here are just a few to get started: We have all sinned against a holy God; lost people matter to God and He loves them; God gave His only Son to die on a cross to offer us cleansing from our sin; we need to confess our sins and ask for God's forgiveness through Christ; God wants to enter a loving and dynamic relationship with us; God has plans for our lives that are exciting and richer than our wildest dreams . . . and the list goes on. The simple truth God has communicated throughout history is still the same today.

SHARPENING THE FOCUS

Read Snapshot "Hearing God Speak Through the Bible" before Question 4

Questions Four & Five Every time you begin a personal Bible study you should say, "Lord, I'm going to read Your Book now, and I want You to speak to me." Every time you have a small group meeting, a discipleship group meeting, or any gathering where the Bible will be opened, begin your group meeting by saying, "Lord, we need a word from You tonight. We pray that this will be more than mechanical. You have spoken in these pages, now we pray that we will hear Your voice." God's Word is powerful and active, and God will speak through it every time it is opened if we have ears to hear.

Read Snapshot "Hearing God Speak Through Preaching and Teaching" before Question 6

Questions Six & Seven Every time you gather with other followers of Christ it is good to pray, "Lord, today I need to hear a word from You. Speak to me through the Scripture reading, through a song, through the message, but speak to me." Come with the expectation that you will receive a word from God.

Another practical suggestion for hearing God speak when you gather with other believers is intentional concentration. Have you ever been driving in your car while listening to a sporting event or radio program and discovered that while you're passing through a particular town the radio station begins to fade or be filled with static? What do you do? You keep turning the volume higher and higher, and you concentrate so you can hear the words through the interference. That same prepared-ness and concentration needs to take place when God's Word is being spoken in a public gathering. It takes discipline to stay focused with the many distractions that can occur.

Another step in hearing God speak is to process what is being said. While a message is being given we need to be committed to honestly evaluate how it relates to us. We need to avoid the pitfall of being overly sensitive and assuming every point is aimed directly at us! We also need to watch out for the temptation to dismiss everything we hear as good advice . . . for someone else!

The final part of listening involves putting what we have learned into action. In the book of James we are warned, "Do not merely listen to the word, and so deceive yourselves. Do what it says" (1:22). Every message we hear from God's Word increases the level of accountability we assume for taking action on what we have heard. We will each be held accountable for the truth we were made aware of and for what we did with it. On one level, if God's words don't impact and change us, we have not really heard them.

Read Snapshot "Hearing God Speak Through the Holy Spirit" before Question 8

Question Eight There are many examples of little ways God speaks to the hearts of His people. Over the years at our church we have had some people who were prompted to improve our landscaping. They were moved by a gentle prompting of the Holy Spirit and they got to work donating equipment, trees, and bushes.

There are all sorts of promptings going on around us. Little nudges and convictions from God. I know it sounds mystical, but they are real. God speaks to His children, from time to time, through His Spirit. "He who has ears, let him hear." And not only do we need to hear those promptings, we need to process them. Make sure they are from God and then act on them. Confess the sin He brings to your heart. Call the person whose name you just can't get out of your mind. Help in the ministry in which He is calling you to participate. As you hear His voice, act on it.

Read Snapshot "Hearing God Speak Through Other People" before Question 9

PUTTING YOURSELF IN THE PICTURE

Challenge group members to take time in the coming week to use part or all of this application section as an opportunity for continued growth.

A NEW VOICE

James 3:3–12

INTRODUCTION

We all need to learn how to control our tongues. This session is about learning the importance of letting the Holy Spirit transform our tongues, voices, and mouths. If you've ever said something that you've regretted, if you've ever "put your foot in your mouth," if you've ever had any difficulty controlling your tongue, this study is for you.

All of us have spoken words we wish we could have taken back. We have also been hurt by the harsh words of others. We know, from personal experience, that words have the power to devastate. On the other hand, we have all experienced the joy and affirmation of hearing someone speak words of encouragement to us. What a powerful experience! God's desire is for us to use our voices to worship Him and build each other up. He wants us to learn how to identify hurtful patterns of speech so we can get them out of our mouths. God wants us to use the awesome power of our voices for good.

THE BIG PICTURE

Take time to read this introduction with the group. There are suggestions for how this can be done in the beginning of this leader's section.

A WIDE ANGLE VIEW

Question One Honest communication in a small group setting about times we have been hurt by the words of others requires deep trust and vulnerability. The second part of this question involves disclosing how our words have hurt others. This could be even more difficult for some group members. However, if we are going to talk about the power of words, we need to get away from vague generalities and discussion about what others have experienced. This session will be most powerful when we can identify the power of our words and the words that others speak to us.

A BIBLICAL PORTRAIT

Read James 3:3–12

Question Two The book of James paints vivid and colorful pictures regarding the power of our voices. James talks about small metal bits in the mouths of horses, rudders on ships, and the damage one spark can do in a dry forest. He is trying to get us to think of a great, powerful stallion—1,200–1,400 pounds of animal—directed wherever the rider wants it to go because of a five-inch piece of metal in its mouth. Remarkable, isn't it? Such a small thing controlling such a large and powerful beast.

Then he says to think of a huge ship, sales billowed out, its mast, halyards, and shrouds straining, but staying on a true course because a helmsman is steering using a small piece of wood or metal at the rear of the ship. A huge ship controlled by a small piece of metal. Isn't it remarkable what a little rudder can do?

Then James invites us to picture a forest fire raging out of control, devouring everything in its path. This whole destructive fire was started from one little careless spark. What James wants us to learn from the bit, the rudder, and the spark, is that the tongue, such a small part of the human anatomy, is just as disproportionately powerful.

Question Three James says, "[The tongue] is a restless evil, full of deadly poison" (3:8). Do you know what it's like to get up in the middle of the night and be restless? You wander around the house. You think you might be hungry or maybe thirsty. You don't know what you want to do, but you can't sit still. James says the tongue is restless . . . just itching to say something. And not only is the tongue restless, but it is "full of deadly poison." The imagery here is of a poisonous snake slithering around with a mouthful of venom looking for someone to bite. James is pretty serious about the dangerous power of the human voice.

SHARPENING THE FOCUS

Read Snapshot "The Power of the Voice . . . to Destroy" before Question 4

Questions Four & Five James 3:9 says, "With the tongue we praise our Lord and Father." This is one of the highest purposes to which we have been called. Our voices can praise, worship, sing, pray, and proclaim the truth of Christ. Yet with these very same voices, we can curse those who just a few minutes earlier we showered with verbal blessings. James says, "and with it we curse men, who have been made in God's likeness." Over the years we have all experienced the damaging effects of harsh words. As we grow up we learn that "sticks and stones may break our bones, but words can break our hearts."

I used to work for an uncle who had a very sharp tongue. I can remember being just seven or eight years old and helping out around the produce business. One day he yelled for me to go get a bag of fruit. I put it on my shoulders, but there was a weak spot in the bottom of the bag. The whole bottom of the bag fell out and the fruit ended up all over the floor. It was purely an accident. I can still remember him screaming, "You idiot!" at the top of his lungs. As a kid, I wanted the men there to see me as a hard worker, a good helper. Those words hurt and humiliated me terribly.

Read Snapshot "The Power of the Voice . . . to Build Up" before Question 6

Questions Six & Seven The power of a compliment given for a small deed of kindness is beyond what most of us realize. We also need to realize the value of statements of affection. People need to hear us tell them how much they mean to us. This kind of speech is rare in today's society, but we need to turn this trend.

God gives us an example of this kind of verbal affirmation in Isaiah 43, one of my favorite passages in Scripture. God says, "You are precious." And now look at His vulnerability. Here's God, the Father, saying, "And I love you. You are precious in My sight. I have called you by name and you are Mine. I love you." It's good for us to be reminded that God loves us. But the key is for us to learn from God's example and to begin to express words of encouragement, affirmation, and blessing.

Unbelievable power for good can be accomplished when you use your tongue constructively. The simple act of encouraging people will make their day. If you compliment them, you can build them up. If you tell them how your heart is filled with love for them, you can impact them for a lifetime.

Read Snapshot "The Power of the Voice . . . to Worship God" before Question 8

PUTTING YOURSELF IN THE PICTURE

Challenge group members to take time in the coming week to use part or all of this application section as an opportunity for continued growth.

NEW HANDS

Proverbs 6:16–17; Ecclesiastes 10:18; Matthew 5:30; Matthew 8:1–4; Luke 18:15–17

INTRODUCTION

We all have a need for new hands. God wants to transform our hands so they are useful for His kingdom. In this session I am going to paint three pictures of our hands. In the "Big Picture" section of this study I tell about the picture of praying hands that was so deeply etched on my mind as I was growing up. The three snapshots that follow describe three different pictures of our hands. I hope each member of your group will seek to use their imagination and try to allow these three pictures to be impressed on their minds.

THE BIG PICTURE

Take time to read this introduction with the group. There are suggestions for how this can be done in the beginning of this leader's section.

A BIBLICAL PORTRAIT

Read Proverbs 6:16–17; Ecclesiastes 10:18; Matthew 5:30

Question Two In the last session we looked at how our voices have great potential for harm as well as for good. This is also true of our hands. Hands can be violent, idle, and as Proverbs reminds us, they can shed blood. Our hands also have the potential to express tenderness, to help others, and to hold things with great tenderness.

These passages remind us of the potential power for evil in our hands. Jesus even went so far as to say that when our hand causes us to sin, we should consider removing it to keep from continuing in this sin. In this passage, Jesus is *not* encouraging the physical mutilation of either our hands or our eyes—sin, after all, has its source in our spirits, not our bodies—but He is saying that the sins we commit with our hands can be so serious that there are times that we need to *live as if we had no hands* if that is what it takes to control them.

79

Read Matthew 8:1–4; Luke 18:15–17

Question Three Take time to read these passages from the gospels of Matthew and Luke. As you read, look for how Jesus used the power of physical touch as He gave sight to the blind, ministered to the outcast, and cared for children. Jesus knew the power of communicating love and care through the touch of a hand. He even reached out and touched those who no one was willing to touch. We need to learn from His example.

SHARPENING THE FOCUS

Read Snapshot "Uplifted Hands" before Question 4

Question Four Lifted hands could symbolize somebody crying out for salvation in Jesus Christ. Outstretched, they say, in effect, "My efforts to merit eternal life will never work. Being a good person won't cut it. Attending church will never cover my sin. My efforts for self-justification just won't measure up. I'm abandoning all of my own works. Oh Lord Jesus, save me." If you have done this, this picture is familiar to you. You can see yourself with hands stretched heavenward saying, "Oh Lord, have mercy on me. Come into my life. Come into my heart."

Question Five Lifted hands can also symbolize an intense prayer of supplication from a believer crying out for help from heaven. In Exodus 17 Moses is up on a mountain overlooking a valley where the Israelites were fighting a battle. They were outnumbered, and things looked bad. Whenever Moses lifted his hands to heaven the army of Israel was victorious. However, when his arms got tired and he lowered them, the Israelites began losing the battle. Thankfully, Moses had two friends with him, Aaron and Hur, who noticed that every time Moses lowered his hands the enemy prevailed. Seeing this, they put a rock under Moses so he could sit, and then each of them took one of Moses' arms and held it up toward heaven. They joined him in crying out to God and the Israelites won the battle. What a wonderful picture of lifting hands to God in prayer!

There are certainly members of your group who have burdens so heavy, challenges so pressing, and grief so deep that they need to lift their hands to heaven for strength to prevail. They might even need other Christians to come alongside of them and help lift their arms, offering prayer and support. We must always remember that God listens to the prayers of His children. Lifting our hands to our heavenly Father and crying out to Him with our needs should be a normal part of our lives as followers of Christ.

Question Six We read that Solomon lifted up his hands toward heaven and began to worship and praise God for the completion of the building of the temple. What a picture! Solomon, the mightiest king on the planet standing before the people in his kingdom, publicly and visibly bestowing honor on the true Ruler of all things, the Almighty King of heaven. Solomon knew what it meant to have people come to his throne and lift up their hands saying, "Long live the king." Now he is saying, "I lift up my hands to the Almighty King."

Read Snapshot "Hand in Hand" before Question 7

Questions Seven & Eight We all have the ability to extend the right hand of fellowship through taking someone's hand during a time of need. Never underestimate the power of a handshake; it communicates something extremely important. As fully devoted followers of Christ, we are freed to reach out beyond ourselves and extend a hand to other Christians. As individuals or a group, we need to commit ourselves to extending a hand to others.

Read Snapshot "Hands on the Plow" before Question 9

Questions Nine & Ten Some people spend their whole lives using their hands to fill their bags with more and more earthly stuff. While these material possessions seem so important, in reality, they are toys and trinkets that won't last many years and certainly won't endure for eternity. God wants us to find real and lasting meaning in life by taking the plow handles of some specific ministry. Every one of us is called to serve God and commit ourselves to using our hands to do His work.

PUTTING YOURSELF IN THE PICTURE

Challenge group members to take time in the coming week to use part or all of this application section as an opportunity for continued growth.

A NEW SPINE

1 Samuel 17:20–51

INTRODUCTION

If you miss the message of this final session, you've missed the whole point of this series of interactions. You see, from the minute you give your heart to Christ, God begins the process of transformation in your life. The Holy Spirit begins to clean house in your heart and life. He begins to root out the old habits and hang-ups. He encourages you to change attitudes and whispers words of warning about behavioral patterns that are no longer appropriate.

For the rest of your life, you will need to make thousands upon thousands of decisions that will help you continue moving forward in the transformation process. In each moment of truth you will have to decide whether or not you will cooperate with the Spirit. Many times every day, you'll come to a moment of truth. You will stand at a crossroad and decide if you have the spine, the courage, to follow God instead of your own desires. This way of courage is the road to transformation.

THE BIG PICTURE

Take time to read this introduction with the group. There are suggestions for how this can be done in the beginning of this leader's section.

A BIBLICAL PORTRAIT

Read Snapshot "A Story of Courage" before Scripture passage

Read 1 Samuel 17:20–51

Questions Two & Three Christianity will demand from you more than you ever dreamed of. The world can go with the flow, but you can't. The world is all going downstream, but God calls you to go upstream. It takes more spine and courage to stand up as a Christian than to do almost anything else in this life. The most courageous people I know are those who have counted the cost and stood for the faith even in a world that rejects the truth of the faith.

I'll never forget talking with a man who had been a follower of Christ for only a few weeks. I had just given a message on telling the truth. At the end of that sermon I said, "Now, if some of you have been involved in telling lies, you need to make it right." The man came up to me afterwards and said, "I'm in big trouble. I just landed a new job. I mean, it's a good job. High salary. More than I've ever made. But I lied in my interview and on my resume. You're not saying that God wants me to tell the truth, are you?"

I said, "God's telling you to go make it right."

He said, "But I went out and bought a new car because I've got a better salary now. This is just going to ruin everything. I know they're going to fire me if I tell the truth."

I said, "Friend, you're at a crossroad. You had better summon the courage to do the right thing, because if you do the right thing, God will reward you. But if you cave in, you will set yourself up for a series of cave-ins over the course of your Christian life. It comes down to this moment. What are you going to do? Are you going to be courageous enough to follow God's leading even if it hurts?"

The man called me later in the week, and said, "I went in and I told the truth." He said, "It was the hardest thing I have ever done in my life, and I don't know what the final result is going to be. But let me tell you something. When I drove out of there, I was a free man." That took courage.

I know of another man who had been a Christian for only a few months when he learned that in order to be a committed believer he couldn't be a part of certain ethical decisions his company had made. The day we talked about it, he took me for a ride in his new Buick Park Avenue his company had just given him. A short time after that, he went in and resigned. He told them he was unwilling to compromise his convictions as a Christian. He didn't have another job lined up, but he knew it was the right thing to do. Don't tell me Christianity is for weaklings and cowards! I know the truth. Christianity is for the courageous!

Sharpening the Focus

Read Snapshot "Believe the Promises of God" before Question 4

Questions Four, Five, & Six Most of us have heard standard lines about Christianity being for weaklings who can't stand on their own two feet. Nothing could be further from the truth. Learning to live out a radical Christian faith in a hostile world takes more courage than any of us has. Not only do we need to use every ounce of our own courage when we are in the furnace of life, but we need to call on the Holy Spirit to grant us extra courage to stay committed to Jesus Christ. Fully devoted followers of Christ will make sacrifices that non-believers would never dare even consider.

Read Snapshot "Living Out the Principles of God" before Question 7

Question Seven Some years ago Lynne and I met a young couple in an airport. The husband had been a Christian for only about six weeks. The couple seemed very excited about the trip they were about to take. When I asked them where they were going, the husband said excitedly, "We're flying to see my folks. They're not Christians, so we're going to tell them all about Jesus. As a matter of fact, we were just praying about it."

Lynne and I responded that that was great, but inside, we were both concerned for this excited young couple.

After the couple had gotten on their plane, I turned to Lynne and said, "Are you thinking what I'm thinking?"

"I fear the worst," she said.

I replied, "I sense a torrential downpour about to soak their picnic. I've seen it again and again. I can just picture that guy walking in and sitting down with his mom and dad and saying, 'Mom and Dad, I'm saved.'"

You see, when this young man's parents heard those words, I knew they would realize they had lost their influence. Their son now had a Lord who would lead and direct his life. When this young man said to them, "I've received forgiveness for my sins through Jesus Christ," his parents would probably think, *That means you think I stand guilty before God.* I could hear that excited young guy saying, "I'm going to heaven when I die," and I could imagine his parents thinking, *So, in your mind, I'm condemned to hell.*

You'd better believe telling others about your faith demands courage. When you say that you're saved, they will figure you're telling them they're lost. This may be true, but they don't like it. If you're forgiven, they're guilty. If you're going to heaven, that means they're going to hell. Because of these contrasts, many people can react adversely to Christians.

They freeze them out, find fault with them, and sometimes even start false rumors about them. It takes courage to stand up as a Christian and keep standing up even when the heat is on.

Questions Eight & Nine It takes a great amount of courage and a strong spine to tell others about your faith. There are even times we know we should say something or do something but we just freeze up. All of us have experienced times when we have looked back and wished we had said something about our faith or acted differently than we did. The purpose of these two questions is not to make people feel bad for the times they have failed to stand up for their faith, but to identify the common things that can stand in the way. When we identify the obstacles and the things that help us communicate our faith, we can begin to strategize about ways to effectively reach those who are seeking Christ.

PUTTING YOURSELF IN THE PICTURE

Challenge group members to take time in the coming week to use part or all of this application section as an opportunity for continued growth.

ADDITIONAL WILLOW CREEK RESOURCES

Small Group Resources

Leading Life-Changing Small Groups, by Bill Donahue and the Willow Creek Small Group Team

The Walking with God series, by Don Cousins and Judson Poling

Evangelism Resources

Becoming a Contagious Christian (book), by Bill Hybels and Mark Mittelberg

Becoming a Contagious Christian (training course), by Mark Mittelberg, Lee Strobel, and Bill Hybels

God's Outrageous Claims, by Lee Strobel

Inside the Mind of Unchurched Harry and Mary, by Lee Strobel

Inside the Soul of a New Generation, by Tim Celek and Dieter Zander, with Patrick Kampert

The Journey: A Bible for Seeking God and Understanding Life

What Jesus Would Say, by Lee Strobel

Spirit Gifts and Ministry

Network (training course), by Bruce Bugbee, Don Cousins, and Bill Hybels

What You Do Best, by Bruce Bugbee

Marriage and Parenting

Fit to Be Tied, by Bill and Lynne Hybels

Authenticity

Honest to God? by Bill Hybels

Descending into Greatness, by Bill Hybels

Ministry Resources

Rediscovering Church, by Bill Hybels

The Source, compiled by Scott Dyer, introduction by Nancy Beach

Sunday Morning Live, edited by Steve Pederson

Christianity 101, by Gilbert Bilezikian

All of these resources are published in association with Zondervan Publishing House.

Willow Creek Association
Vision, Training, Resources for Prevailing Churches

This resource was created to serve you and to help you in building a local church that prevails!

Since 1992, the Willow Creek Association (WCA) has been linking like-minded, action-oriented churches with each other and with strategic vision, training, and resources. Now a worldwide network of over 6,400 churches from more than ninety denominations, the WCA works to equip Member Churches and others with the tools needed to build prevailing churches. Our desire is to inspire, equip, and encourage Christian leaders to build biblically functioning churches that reach increasing numbers of unchurched people, not just with innovations from Willow Creek Community Church in South Barrington, Illinois, but from any church in the world that has experienced God-given breakthroughs.

WILLOW CREEK CONFERENCES

Each year, thousands of local church leaders, staff and volunteers—from WCA Member Churches and others—attend one of our conferences or training events. Conferences offered on the Willow Creek campus in South Barrington, Illinois, include:

Prevailing Church Conference: Foundational training for staff and volunteers working to build a prevailing local church.

Prevailing Church Workshops: More than fifty strategic, day-long workshops covering seven topic areas that represent key characteristics of a prevailing church; offered twice each year.

Promiseland Conference: Children's ministries; infant through fifth grade.

Student Ministries Conference: Junior and senior high ministries.

Willow Creek Arts Conference: Vision and training for Christian artists using their gifts in the ministries of local churches.

Leadership Summit: Envisioning and equipping Christians with leadership gifts and responsibilities; broadcast live via satellite to eighteen cities across North America.

Contagious Evangelism Conference: Encouragement and training for churches and church leaders who want to be strategic in reaching lost people for Christ.

Small Groups Conference: Exploring how developing a church *of* small groups can play a vital role in developing authentic Christian community that leads to spiritual transformation.

To find out more about WCA conferences, visit our website at www.willowcreek.com.

PREVAILING CHURCH REGIONAL WORKSHOPS

Each year the WCA team leads several, two-day training events in select cities across the United States. Some twenty day-long workshops are offered in topic areas including leadership, next-generation ministries, small groups, arts and worship, evangelism, spiritual gifts, financial stewardship, and spiritual formation. These events make quality training more accessible and affordable to larger groups of staff and volunteers.

To find out more about Prevailing Church Regional Workshops, visit our website at www.willowcreek.com.

WILLOW CREEK RESOURCES™

Churches can look to Willow Creek Resources™ for a trusted channel of ministry tools in areas of leadership, evangelism, spiritual gifts, small groups, drama, contemporary music, financial stewardship, spiritual transformation, and more. For ordering information, call (800) 570-9812 or visit our website at www.willowcreek.com.

WCA MEMBERSHIP

Membership in the Willow Creek Association as well as attendance at WCA Conferences is for churches, ministries, and leaders who hold to a historic, orthodox understanding of biblical Christianity. The annual church membership fee of $249 provides substantial discounts for your entire team on all conferences and Willow Creek Resources, networking opportunities with other outreach-oriented churches, a bimonthly newsletter, a subscription to the *Defining Moments* monthly audio journal for leaders, and more.

To find out more about WCA membership, visit our website at www.willowcreek.com.

WILLOWNET (WWW.WILLOWCREEK.COM)

This Internet resource service provides access to hundreds of Willow Creek messages, drama scripts, songs, videos, and multimedia ideas. The system allows you to sort through these elements and download them for a fee.

Our website also provides detailed information on the Willow Creek Association, Willow Creek Community Church, WCA membership, conferences, training events, resources, and more.

WILLOWCHARTS.COM (WWW.WILLOWCHARTS.COM)

Designed for local church worship leaders and musicians, WillowCharts.com provides online access to hundreds of music charts and chart components, including choir, orchestral, and horn sections, as well as rehearsal tracks and video streaming of Willow Creek Community Church performances.

THE NET (HTTP://STUDENTMINISTRY.WILLOWCREEK.COM)

The NET is an online training and resource center designed by and for student ministry leaders. It provides an inside look at the structure, vision, and mission of prevailing student ministries from around the world. The NET gives leaders access to complete programming elements, including message outlines, dramas, small group questions, and more. An indispensable resource and networking tool for prevailing student ministry leaders!

CONTACT THE WILLOW CREEK ASSOCIATION

If you have comments or questions, or would like to find out more about WCA events or resources, please contact us:

Willow Creek Association
P.O. Box 3188, Barrington, IL 60011-3188
Phone: (800) 570-9812 or (847) 765-0070
Fax (888) 922-0035 or (847) 765-5046
Web: www.willowcreek.com

More life-changing small group discussion guides from Willow Creek

Walking with God Series

Don Cousins and Judson Poling

This series of six guides (and two leader's guides) provides a solid, biblical program of study for all of the small groups in your church. The Walking with God Series is designed to help lead new and young believers into a deeper personal intimacy with God, while at the same time building a strong foundation in the faith for all believers, regardless of their level of maturity. These guides are also appropriate for individual study. Titles in the series are:

Friendship with God: Developing Intimacy with God: 0-310-59143-0
The Incomparable Jesus: Experiencing the Power of Christ: 0-310-59153-8
"Follow Me!": Walking with Jesus in Everyday Life: 0-310-59163-5
Leader's Guide 1 (covers these first three books): 0-310-59203-8
Discovering Your Church: Becoming Part of God's New Community: 0-310-59173-2
Building Your Church: Using Your Gifts, Time, and Resources: 0-310-59183-X
Impacting Your World: Becoming a Person of Influence: 0-310-59193-7
Leader's Guide 2 (covers these last three books): 0-310-59213-5

*Look for the Walking with God Series
at your local Christian bookstore.*

GRAND RAPIDS, MICHIGAN 49530

w w w . z o n d e r v a n . c o m

More insights on following Christ's example of radical love

Descending Into Greatness

Bill Hybels and Rob Wilkins

In a society where "upward mobility" is the highest goal, Bill Hybels asks a tough question: Do Christians place God's desires first, or their own? In *Descending Into Greatness,* he and Rob Wilkins look at the example of Christ's downward journey as the radical and essential model for every Christian's life. Moving down is never easy. It requires a life committed to discipleship. But the rewards are worth it, as illustrated in the book's moving and inspiring true-life stories. As Hybels and Wilkins write, "Like Christ, we must descend—into self-abandonment, unconditional giving, sacrifice, and death to self. And, like Christ, we will then ascend—into fulfillment, blessing, joy, and purpose."

Softcover: 0-310-54471-8

Look for Descending Into Greatness
at your local Christian bookstore.

ZONDERVAN

GRAND RAPIDS, MICHIGAN 49530
www.zondervan.com

WILLOW CREEK
RESOURCES

Amazing Insights into the Christian Life

God's Outrageous Claims

Thirteen Discoveries That Can Revolutionize Your Life

Lee Strobel

Sometimes God says things that seem absolutely outrageous. What's more, He wants to do astonishing things in us and through us—if we're willing to take what He says seriously. In *God's Outrageous Claims,* Lee Strobel investigates thirteen phenomenal claims that the Bible makes, along the way challenging us to allow these revolutionary claims to transform our lives. Strobel says, "If we take these claims seriously and open ourselves to God's activity, we discover new insights into who we are and new principles that show how we can live with courage and conviction."

Hardcover: 0-310-20929-3
Also available on audio cassette: 0-310-21194-8

Look for God's Outrageous Claims
at your favorite bookstore.

GRAND RAPIDS, MICHIGAN 49530
www.zondervan.com

WILLOW CREEK RESOURCES

We want to hear from you. Please send your comments about this book to us in care of the address below. Thank you.

GRAND RAPIDS, MICHIGAN 49530

WWW.ZONDERVAN.COM